CALIFORNIA MAN LEGALLY DESIGNS HIS OWN DEATH

A Southern California couple survives dangerous, far-flung travel and a global pandemic only to discover a rare, deadly disease will change the course of their lives.

A story of love, heartbreak, strength, personal choice, and the fortitude of one woman who walked her husband to the doors of death and kept on walking.

LIVING WITH VERACITY
DYING WITH DIGNITY

LIVING with VERACITY
DYING with DIGNITY

ALISON CLAY-DUBOFF

atmosphere press

This book is dedicated to my late husband Ken Duboff whose absolute presence in my life gave me endless, profound, unimaginable joy.

CHAPTER 1
THE JOURNEY

My husband was the bravest man I'll ever know. I will be in awe of his courage for the rest of my earthly days. This is Ken's story about a very personal choice, his own death.

Ken was a ravenous consumer of all things 'life'. I have been retelling the tales of Ken's travel adventures for decades, how he hitchhiked across Europe, mastered Russia and formed his own KGB (Ken's Good Bank) and experienced the Middle East, all the while collecting experiences and a wife here and there. On many a Gin and Tonic evening by our fire he explained the importance of the perfect travel partner and how those same qualities were necessary for the perfect life partner. At the age of forty-nine, Ken finally found his perfect travel and life partner. I was the lucky recipient of his good fortune.

I too had been searching for my missing half. Widowed at thirty-six with a nine-year-old daughter, I had no idea who was waiting on the wings of my future. The stars aligned, our fates collided, we blended our families and eventually, when we cast the adult children off on their life paths, far-flung adventures became our passion.

India is unlike any other country, intense and mysterious. We fell in love with its people, the diverse landscapes and for me, the food. However, India isn't an easy country or populous to digest. India is as 'in your face' as it gets. Ironically Ken and I loved everything we hated about mother India; the noise, the traffic, the smog. India got under our skin.

Taj Mahal

Our first trip was definitely eye-opening even though we both had traveled extensively in the Middle East and I had lived in Saudi Arabia for three years. This India trip was a huge bucket list item for me. A very dear friend lived in Mumbai, and my earnest wish was to cast my eyes upon him once again. Ken prided himself on making my dreams come true, and he turned many into reality.

Not long after our trip to India and in-between a few other adventures, Ken learned about a religious festival that was coming up in 2019. It's called Kumbh Mela, and the name itself strikes fear even in Indian's own hearts. It's known as the world's largest peaceful gathering of humanity on planet earth, where a hundred and fifty million souls gather at the Ganges over three months for their rituals of spiritual cleansing and attaining Moksha, 'the transcendent state attained as a result of being released from the cycle of rebirth'.

Historically the pilgrimage had been plagued with catastrophes; stampedes, fire, illness; they had all occurred in past Kumbh's. None of these real potential death traps diluted Ken's desire to attend.

This type of India trip was not on my bucket list. My lackluster interest didn't put a dent in Ken's enthusiasm. He was committed to the idea of attending this unimaginable pilgrimage. I had to ask if he was truly serious, so one night, I off-handedly asked him how important was this trip to him on a scale of one to ten. He answered without hesitation and with utter earnestness. **It was a resounding ten**. What could I say to that? What could I say to my person whose main goal in life was to make me happy? Only one phrase: "BOOK IT."

I couldn't believe we were going back to India. India is dirty, loud, polluted yet totally magical. But this wouldn't be a vacation. No Taj Mahal, no fortresses or palaces. It would be an intense experiential life-altering event. It took me some time to grow my enthusiasm, but very soon I was all in.

Ken was muscular, fit from years of racquet ball and cycling. We had a tandem bike and would ride for hours on the weekends to the tip top of the Palos Verdes Peninsula and back home to Redondo Beach, about seventeen miles round trip. This Kumbh Mela pilgrimage required intense stamina. There would be hours of long walks through tent cities and campfires to the different religious events. The air would be thick with incense and smoke.

Ken, who had since retired, lived to travel. He spent hours on the internet researching and interviewing travel companies until he had arranged a deluxe 'glamping' experience. Safe, secure, 'hygienic' with healthy food and luxurious accommodations, it sounded idyllic and comforting.

Upon arrival in Mumbai in December of 2019, I got sick again. A nagging viral upper respiratory infection took its toll. The flights and subsequent drive to the temporary "MegaCity" was nearly intolerable for me, but Ken was glowing with jubilation and excitement. After hours of driving at a snail's pace, getting lost, and our guide frustrated and irritable; we finally arrived at our camp site; it was indeed something to behold. Pathways lit with shimmering lanterns, a mini tent city spilled out in front of us with carpeted walkways, tents zipped up with foreigners from all over the globe tucked inside. We met a couple from Hermosa Beach, one village from our home in California in this most remote, temporary and bizarre spot on the globe. It was unreal.

It turned out it was a good thing I got so sick. The hikes were flat but grueling. The smoke, dust, humanity and incense was choking. Hours of walking. After one half day of that, I retreated to the tent for the remainder of the trip. Ken was deeply relieved I wasn't able to be with him in the midst of the huge throng of humanity. His worry for my safety would have inhibited his experience. He was very protective, in the best of ways. And, this was 'his' experience, not mine. I was happy to live this vicariously through him from the comfort of our tent. I tracked his path from my cell phone in-between bouts of fever. At certain intervals I lost contact altogether. It was unnerving. He walked through the night, and by morning I had heated thirty-plus little tea pots of hot water and filled him a makeshift bath. He was cleansed, but his jacket and cap were never to be washed, EVER.

After surviving a surreal Kumbh Mela experience, we closed that chapter, however, Ken couldn't wait to go back. It breaks my heart that the next time I will be in his beloved India, it will be to scatter his ashes in the Ganges.

The next travel location of 2020 was to be an adventure of my choosing, and I chose Peru. I had had Shirley McClain infused dreams of Machu Picchu since I was in University and Ken's goal in life, so he told me often, was to make me happy, and he never disappointed.

We went to Peru in March 2020 on the heels of Covid. Our friends and family were appalled by our brazen attitude. We assured them we would be fine. Unfortunately or fortunately, a different adventure awaited us, like a cobra waiting to strike.

After two bewitching and beguiling days on the Amazon river, the Clarke family of three, the only other guests, Ken and I marveled at the flora and fauna, wild macaws and a pod of elusive pink dolphins. We visited a monkey habitat (I got to cuddle a baby sloth), a small village's peoples, their culture and their handicrafts; the trip took an ugly turn. We were awoken in the middle of the night by the owner of the boat and his security detail. We stood in the hallway in our terrycloth robes and slippers. We were told The Peruvian President was going to close the country's borders in twelve hours, and after that we would no longer be allowed off the boat. We would be effectively quarantined prisoners aboard. Decisions had to be made quickly and unanimously.

It was the twilight of a global pandemic. If we wanted to leave the country, there wasn't much chance unless we motored through the night in a small skiff to Iquitos, where we had boarded just forty-eight hours before, in an attempt to catch a flight. The chances were beyond remote, and Mr. Clarke Sr. was in his 80s and was not in a position for such an arduous journey. Or, we could stay aboard and work on getting a Mercy flight home.

To do that, we would have to travel all night in the boat, and pirates would have easy access in the dark of night. Again Ken proved to be my hero, my courageous, hilarious and wonderful husband. We all decided to risk the night travel and head to Iquitos. At daybreak, the military attempted to board our vessel. The owner would not allow them access, so in return, we five passengers were not permitted to leave the boat, and the boat was not allowed to move from the very unscenic spot where we had docked in the early hours. This beautiful wooden vessel was a sitting duck in this location, and the situation had the potential to turn dark and dangerous at any moment. We were running low on provisions (so were the locals), but we were guarded by armed staff that patrolled by night. Ironic as it sounds, by day we were making Pisco Sours in a cocktail class, having endless massages and laughing to camouflage the fear. I believe Ken relished every moment.

Our eventual evacuation by the State Department two weeks later was like a scene out of a Tarantino movie. The streets were in utter chaos. Our hired van had a private motorcycle escort, a veritable Amazonian woman about six feet tall, leather boots and a very serious demeanor. We passed lines of locals waiting to buy food. The banks were closed. People held up signs begging the President to help them. It was the first time I'd felt actual fear.

The situation at the airport was pure science fiction. There were hundreds of stranded foreigners. Some recognized each other from the various 'Stuck in Iquitos' Facebook groups. The airline staff was dressed head to toe in protective gear. None spoke English. We had to take medical exams, blood pressure and throat checks. Mr. Clarke Sr's bp was sky-high. The restrooms were not working, the lights were off, there was no ventilation. This was not normal operations at the airport. The flights were for foreigners to get home.

At check-in, Mr. Clark Sr.'s name was not on the manifest. True panic ensued. His son and daughter-in-law would not leave him there, nor would we. We were bound together. Luckily, with forceful body language and a few calls, we all passed and went through security. We could see the planes on the tarmac. At last, the Latam crew came through, and they received a standing ovation. It was very emotional. We were going home.

Living it up during quarantine in Peru

Once back home we were local celebrities. The tale of the Duboff's was in the Wall Street Journal, local papers and all over the internet. It was good to be home. We had two new adventures waiting in the wings. A new puppy and bad news.

Our *"Toes Up House"*

"The Boos"

On the Amazon

Glamping at Kumbh Mela

Ken's Kumbh Mela Adventure

CHAPTER 2
THE DECLINE

Ken hadn't felt well since his birthday in Peru on March 13, 2020. He had general malaise, breathing issues we attributed to his normal seasonal asthma. But then his health started to really decline.

In the weird pandemic of June 2020, we were handed some bad news – Ken had non-Hodgkin's Bonemarrow Lymphoma. A very rare disease that was found by semi-annual blood tracking. The good news was the disease, Waldenstrom Syndrome was extremely indolent. The oncologist assured us treatment was not necessary and something *else* would eventually kill Ken.

As the days, weeks and months passed, Ken was having worsening breathing issues, he began stuttering. He had severe stomach issues. We were told emphatically none of those symptoms were related to his Lymphoma. We wondered if he caught some rare parasite in the Amazon? Some bizarre virus or amoeba on our trips to India? He always refused to use bottled water to brush his teeth. I wanted to kill him at the time. Oh, hindsight, you are a bitch.

More days and weeks passed. Ken's breathing became further disrupted – he had less stamina. He had a hard time catching his breath. His stomach was increasingly problematic and painful. His speech was a struggle. His feet turned purple and spotty. His symptoms were so varied there was no real path to identify what ailed him.

We spent the next fifteen months searching for a diagnosis; Ken endured every test filled with hope and patience. Painful EMGs, literally hundreds of blood draws, multiple upper and lower endoscopies, infectious disease doctors with invasive ENT scopes, CT Scans, chest X-rays, MRIs and more. Nothing was perceivable. There were some strange shadows around his kidneys but no apparent cause. I had lengthy conversations with the medical practitioners. The doctors were impressed with my grasp of medicine. The feeling wasn't mutual. I doubted the specialists. Couldn't they see my husband was dying?

The oncologist suggested Ken try 'Imbruvica', a specific lymphoma treatment. But after two doses it threw Ken's heart into A-flutter, which required a hospital procedure called an Ablation and and overnight stay during Covid. He spent the night alone in a glowing hospital room. This hospital stay wasn't his first over our life together, and I was always right at his side, asleep in the chair or bed next to him. Not this time.

Imbruvica was out. No more hope on that front.

The Doctors and Specialists from UCLA, Little Company of Mary, Private Practice (one Doctor told Ken the only thing wrong with him was unresolved father issues) found nothing. The Waldenstrom (his type of lymphoma) Specialist Doctor with The Mayo Clinic in Phoenix said, "Ken, I can't help you. However, I know a Hematologist at the Mayo Clinic in Minnesota who takes on oddball cases, and you are definitely an oddball case; would you like a referral?"

We were delivered a death sentence a scant twelve hours after our arrival in Minnesota. A few simple tests definitively revealed what hundreds could not.

The Hematologist's explanation was as follows:

"Doctors are taught 'when you hear hoofbeats, think horses not zebras,' meaning **a doctor should first think about what is a more common—and potentially more likely—diagnosis**...

Ken had a diagnosis at last, however not what we hung our hopes upon. It was the worst possible outcome, the worst possible prognosis.

It was terminal end-stage Congestive Heart failure due to AL Amyloidosis. The disease being very advanced, had already destroyed his heart, his gut, and to some degree, his speech. There was possible neurological involvement. His life expectancy was curt. Right there and then he insisted the doctors tell him exactly how he would die. I was mortified by his questioning. The different scenarios were ugly. Congestive heart failure was death by suffocation, or a cardiac arrhythmia that could take him out at any moment – and that one was the best scenario. Total devastation weighed down upon us in the bland Mayo Clinic office. He (we), had six months or less. I watched Ken's shoulders sink into a bottomless abyss in the floor. My heart was disintegrating as I planned out the next few hours, weeks... I knew I had a herculean undertaking ahead. But I had to be the strong one, the positive essence in his remaining days. I had to be wife, partner, mother and advocate. I tried to be upbeat yet sobbed in the privacy of the bathroom.

The Mayo Clinic is indeed all it is billed up to be. They use a fully integrated holistic approach of analysis and testing; all the doctors on a patient's care team work together; not like the fragmented way most hospital groups operate. Ken described Mayo's approach as "all the doctors sit around a smoky poker table and discuss Ken Duboff." And the structure works.

Ken's eldest son Scott flew to Minnesota to be at his father's side. Ken's illness proffered a reason to reconnect after a long rupture in their relationship. Some clouds have silver linings. I was grateful for their reunion.

Defeated and exhausted, we retreated home to sunny California. It was to be our last flight together, one we never ever could or would have imagined.

By the time we returned to Redondo Beach our home was outfitted with grab bars, a wheelchair ramp and a walker. It was preposterous to think just one month prior Ken was playing paddle tennis, walking our two huge Bouvier des Flandres dogs, each weighing in at 90+Lbs each.

Back at home our nightly routines took on new patterns. We would sit in almost utter silence as Ken tried to catch his breath, to steady his breathing. My role was to be quiet, to keep the dogs quiet. The tension was palpable, thick and tarry. The nightly triage of blood pressure checks and pulse readings were followed with cocktails by the fire. It was a surreal existence, to say the least. I couldn't fathom what was going through his mind, what was his heart telling him, what, more importantly, was he NOT telling *me*.

I knew Ken was suffering, emotionally and physically, but I was suffering too. I carried the blunt force trauma of our new life. Soon I was on the receiving end of the worst of him. I was no longer his priority, my role now was of caregiver.

Life is fickle. Life is messy. Life is humbling yet beautiful. Searching for answers, seeking the light, straining for relief from the relentless clawing for normalcy I carry forth.

Ken's deterioration was not forgiving. I sat demurely and watched, paying witness to his suffering and accepted I was powerless to his suffering. The slow vanishing, the disappearance and diminishing of his physical self, molecule by molecule, atom by atom as he was evaporating. I tried to hold onto him like a helium balloon, hoping he wouldn't float away from my grasp, but he was. It was my nightmarish reality.

He suffered from severe ortho static hypotension. Upon standing, he would black out, falling into my arms as I tried to guide him to the floor in safety. The strong (what I felt unnecessary) dose of Gabapentin for his infrequent electric shooting limb pain gave him hallucinations. Life was more than we both could manage or ever imagine. I wondered, fatigued and depressed, how the hell did we get there?

Watching Ken decline in slow motion destroyed my fortitude. I struggled to inhabit the present, not to focus upon his raking cough, but instead to bask in his words, "I love you, Alison." For those moments, I had him. He was still mine, but I knew he was slipping through my fingers like liquid sadness, handfuls of tears.

At the suggestion of the oncologist, Ken tried one more round of Chemo, but the meds were ineffectual and stole what remained of his stamina. He landed in the hospital for a week due to increasingly frequent blackouts that are sadly etched in my memory.

I spent my days at the hospital by his side, most often in shared silence. I'd go home to sleep and rush back to be at his side as soon as I was able. Covid visiting hours were still limited.

In the hospital, Ken stopped eating. It wasn't just the hospital food; it was Ken. I tried to lure him with his favorite junk foods, Tito's, McDonald's, Grande Mocha Frappuccino with Whip - Nothing appealed to him. Ken simply lost his will to eat.

The Doctors told him that his days would be vastly curtailed if he didn't eat. Ken said he wasn't ready to die. He didn't want feeding tubes. The I.V. nourishment we tried wasn't being absorbed, and he began swelling. His body rejected the nourishment. We had deep, long conversations with the hospital nutritionist doctor. He was frank, honest and told Ken to go home, eat whatever he wanted and enjoy what time he had left. Blunt, and to the point.

We were forced to face a dreaded fork in the road. Fight or go home. We chose to go home, to go home to die. We chose Hospice.

Within six hours of Ken's decision to retreat to the warm embrace of our home, plans were set in unstoppable motion. Hospice is a well-oiled machine. Our house was quickly consumed with all the things hospice; hospital bed, 'comfort kit' with Morphine, Lorazepam, Haldol, laxatives, adult 'undergarments', bed liners, all the usual paraphernalia. It was an astonishing precision maneuver. The only problem was when Ken was delivered home via medical ambulance; he refused the hospital bed. He was not emotionally ready for the hospital bed even though his body truly was.

Everyone in this position of helplessness merits some semblance of agency. Ken was no exception, so I relented (not that I had much choice), and we spent the first few nights together in our marital bed. It was a disaster and was clearly unsustainable. Our life quickly moved into our unrecognizable living room where the reviled hospital bed awaited. I became best friends with our couch, my own hospital bed of sorts. I slept there for the remainder of his life, positioned without more than a millimeter of space between us.

I tried consciously to be acutely careful with my visible feelings of hopelessness. If I slipped and unwittingly revealed my despair, it would make him cry. I would hate myself for it. He would hate himself for making me cry, saying he was a monster. I struggled to be the rock of Gibraltar full of positivity, but often my resolve would crumble under the weight of total fear. Staying sane was near impossible.

Ken was becoming a slighter version of himself. I missed his smile, his reckless mischievousness. But at least I could reach over and touch his skin, smell his hair, listen to his breath. How I wish I could do that today.

Our two dogs Babu the covid puppy and I.V., the female from Ken's hospitalization in Paris (another story), were suffering too. They had been staying at the Kennel across from the hospital during Ken's stay. Babu, the puppy, was grieving deeply. Prior to Ken being diagnosed, our eldest Bouvier Argus decided to pass on his own. He knew his master was sick; they both suffered from Lymphoma. Argus the magnificent just checked out. He was eleven years old and died suddenly at the Vets. Another blow, another loss. Baby Babu was pining for his big brother, who taught him all the tricks, and how to be a man dog. Our home was reeking of sadness. The dogs didn't understand the hospital bed, the quiet, the palpable stress.

Outside the walls of our home, the community rallied around us. Neighbors cooked, visited, checked in. But most amazingly, the community of strangers truly stepped up. I had been positing my sad musings on NextDoor, and the response was overwhelmingly positive. Love poured out from every corner of our neighborhood and continues to this day.

Ken had retired five years prior. He loved it. I was and still am a full-time realtor. He was the ideal house husband, he did the marketing, the laundry, the dog walking, dinner preparation, he was also an integral part of my business. For the last five years I barely had any domestic duties. Life was blissful. I worked damn hard, but Ken was my muse. Suddenly I had assumed all household responsibilities. It was overwhelming. Life as we knew it had stopped in its tracks. I never left his side, and I couldn't leave the house. I refused to leave his side. I was in overdrive.

I ordered online groceries, hired a dog walker (generously sponsored by my community), did the laundry and revisited diaper changing for the first time in thirty-one years. I became an expert on condom catheters; Ken might disagree if he were still alive. We were being tested, it seemed. Ken was depressed, challenging, he was snippy, short-tempered, and then he would weep, asking why he was so awful to me. I could only attempt to assuage his sadness. He was willful, determined to be his own man when in reality, he knew he was only a shadow of his former masculine self.

The only remedy was twenty-four-hour caregiving. I needed to be his wife.

Home health help is extremely expensive. Some of the business owners operate like pimps. Often these individuals who lovingly care for others with empathy, gentle kindness and honor often don't receive the same in return from their employers. They

Pure Love

work without contracts and are subject to the whims of their bosses. That is another story indeed, it needs to be a documentary if it's not already.

Ken's needs became too much for me alone; I needed help. As much as I tried to resist and to admit it, I was sinking fast. I knew it was time for help when my diet consisted of Kraft Mac n Cheese microwave cups for breakfast, lunch and dinner.

Not soon enough, and after a few failed attempts, our house grew by two, JoJo and Floyd, Ken's wonderful Caregivers.

I don't know how I could have survived without them, and they changed my life forever.

Then there was the cost; at that time in someone's illness, terminal illness on Hospice, the duration of twenty-four-hour care is uncertain. But at a minimum calculation, the cost was upward of $12,000 a month. Long Term Care Insurance, that's a topic that needs to be explored for those of you looking to protect yourself from financial ruin.

Ken was told in Minnesota that he would never drive again. Another devastating blow to his ego and his love of his 911 Cab Convertible, black on black that I had bought him many years before. It was time to sell it for his continued care.

This task was made easier by a dear friend who was also a Porsche enthusiast. She placed the car on Auto Trader, and it sold within hours.

As I cleaned out the car, I wept openly and uncontrollably, looking at each hotel key card Ken kept. All the memories, countless road trips, never more, never more.

Ken interrupted my selfish sobbing with urgent instructions. I was told to place my huge red bow and 'Sold Sign' on the car and to wipe away any smudges or fingerprints. There I was feeling so sorry for myself, and Ken wanted to surprise the new owner and make him happy. That's who Ken was inside and out.

With two new personalities in our small Craftsman home, it wasn't exactly smooth sailing at first. JoJo sang cheery tunes with her heavy Philippine accent, and it drove Ken to distraction. He would loudly ask me to tell her to stop singing. I would cringe, conflicted. Floyd snored like a herd of buffalos at night and had to be relocated downstairs, which was too far away from where I needed him in the middle of the night. Ken would need an adult garment change, and Floyd didn't awake to my constant texts. I would climb out from the couch like some Cirque de Soleil acrobat and make my way down to Floyd, who awoke, disheveled and cheery and always ready to wipe Ken's butt with a smile.

Eventually, we all found our mutual rhythm, our common ground, and we triumphed for Ken together.

The caregiver duties of JoJo and Floyd seldom varied. There was morning care which consisted of fresh OJ followed by coffee, then vitals, meds administered by me (I'm a control freak), a catheter bag change, teeth brushing and a sponge bath. Seemly always shortly thereafter, the Hospice Nurse would arrive, and most of that process would be repeated.

As time progressed and relationships developed, Ken started bossing Floyd, asking him to cook Philippine dishes, which Floyd did with great panache. It was very much outside of his usual caregiving duties, yet he would sing in the kitchen while Ken and I would laugh. Ken also came to love JoJo's singing; it soothed him where once it irritated him. There was a certain beauty in this life, like a soft pastel painting, slightly blurry, out of focus.

Hospice was vastly different from what I had imagined. It was surprisingly hectic and routine. It appeared more military than humanitarian. Daily and upon arrival of the Hospice nurse there was no time for small talk. Vitals had to be checked, supplies to be calculated and ordered, skin to be checked for bed sores, anxiety levels to be assessed, medication to be reassessed and ordered as needed.

Hospice meds are very constipating and that causes horrible anxiety. Ken didn't want meds but he needed them; coaxing from the nurses helped somewhat. It's difficult for a grown man to take a crap in a diaper lying down. It's even harder to take a crap in a diaper in bed when you are horribly backed up. Once when Ken was desperately straining, he started to cry. It was horrible to witness. He was literally trying to give birth to a bowel movement and it was consuming his life force. Floyd, who was helping, said, "Hey baby doll, why are you crying?" at which point Ken pivoted from crying to laughing. I succumbed into hysterics, grateful for Floyd's perfect timing. I wonder to this day if it was an intentional comment to defuse Ken's tearful anxiety or just Floyd being Floyd. Some mysteries are better left unsolved.

Hospice nurses are angels on earth. They have more patients than they can adequately manage. The vital time for human interaction gets relegated to the back seat due to the sheer number of patients they must tend to. Ken's hospice bather regularly didn't have time to eat. I would make Hiromi lunch bags to go with nuts, fruit, whatever I could muster. She was the most gentle, loving carer. She truly loved Ken, and he loved her. Our Health Care system is broken when our caregivers can't care for themselves.

After a long day of Life on Hospice, Ken would have his nighttime regimen. I would administer his meds after he carefully examined each pill. I would clean his morphine syringe with water, and Floyd or JoJo would clean him up, and we'd be ready for bed. We'd talk quietly, play footsies through the metal bars, hold hands and he'd fall asleep. I'd take to my cell phone, writing what would one day become this book.

I wrote these words one night while Ken slept next to me, cold metal rails separating us.

Our house is upside down, our hearts are inside out. Life on Hospice is a unique existence, surreal and bewildering.

Clean sheets and supplies fill every corner, our living room is transformed into a small hospital, grieving center, and reflective space.

Chaos is the unwelcome visitor. Nurses, caregivers – don't they know I'm climbing a mountainous task of creating a quiet, peaceful space for my beloved to overcome his fears, his anguish, his sentiments that his life has been ripped away from his grasp?

The dogs whimper and pace in tune with the anxiety, stress permeating and suffocating us all.

Our house is 'cozy', a synonym for small. Tight corners make for difficult shifting of people, supplies and hygiene.

Life is lived in question marks – how long, how do we actually move through this, along this path with grace, dignity and confidence?

The burden is so pendulous – how to create lightness?
The heaviness in this task takes my breath away, renders
me unraveled.

The love, support of our community, our friends and total
strangers is the light in my dark, the strength in my weak
moments and the smile on my lips.

Hospice – you are indeed a double-edged dagger.

The sound of Hospice is a melody unique and perplexing,
comforting and unnerving. The hum and bubbling clank of
the oxygen machine, the snoring of the caregivers, the
nervous barking of the dogs and the loud thumping of my
heart create a somber sonata. The ticking and gonging of
our grandfather clock and the dripping of the sink are the
backup chorus.

The habitual harmonics never vary. The scooping and
scratching of Ice from the freezer, dishes being rinsed
seemingly endlessly. The singing of the microwave, the
beat of the dryer running 24/7.

Hospice harmony sometimes happens by surprise
when laughter, happy tears and the voices of family and
neighbors fill the void where normality once resided.

My soul has shifted. I'm learning about Ken's self-
views I never knew. Revelations startle and unsettle my
fleeting ease. He's Inhabiting, engulfed in moments of
anguish and self-doubt. As I listen to his tears, time heats
to elasticity. This suspended, upended time renders me
torn.

I ache with the belief that no one should ever endure
such emotional, physical, uncut raw pain – and yet – I feel
everyone should. There are snow-covered mountain peaks
of learning within this pain, through this suffering.

Perhaps now, as Ken's life is drawing closer to his
earthly end, our twenty-plus years of memories will be my
pot of gold at the end of Ken's rainbow, and I hope Ken's
will be something indescribably beautiful on the other
side.

A cascade of consonants tumble from the deep grey matter of my mind as my errant tears make tracks upon my cheeks.

As if on a split-screen, I see my husband's muscles flail under their crepe paper skin enclosure, almost shimmering in their electronic dance, whilst I visualize my heart slowly splintering into sharp shards that hurt, stab and scrape.

How is it possible to feel so alone in the same space with someone I love so deeply? His tired breaths reassure me of his present presence, but the absence of his previous self, starved by disease, eats away at my resolve. My fortitude is as ephemeral as the tips of dandelion flowers. I am fierce and resolute, yet in a flash, I'm a silent whimpering puddle of weakness.

This path, my journey, my beloved's journey do not align, do not merge into the sun setting on our horizon as planned. Our paths are slapped, stolen and redirected away from one another. Our agony knows no bounds.

Ken's body is failing. My love for him is attempting to prop us both up, to bring in another day, another sunrise, another moment, another memory. But I can not save him. He's drowning in his own body, turning inward, lips trembling, a secret language I strain to understand. His limbs conduct an invisible orchestra of otherworldly melodies.

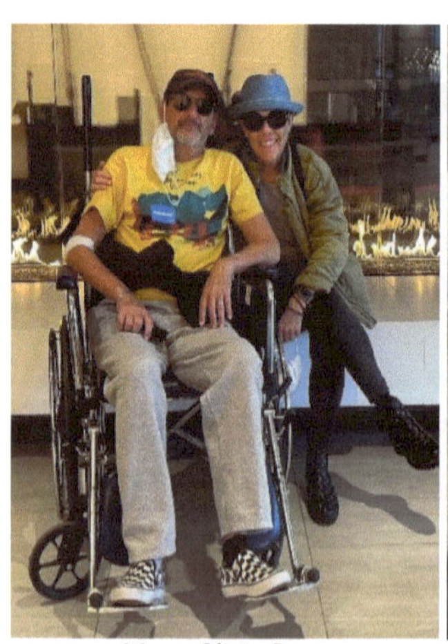

Mayo Clinic Days

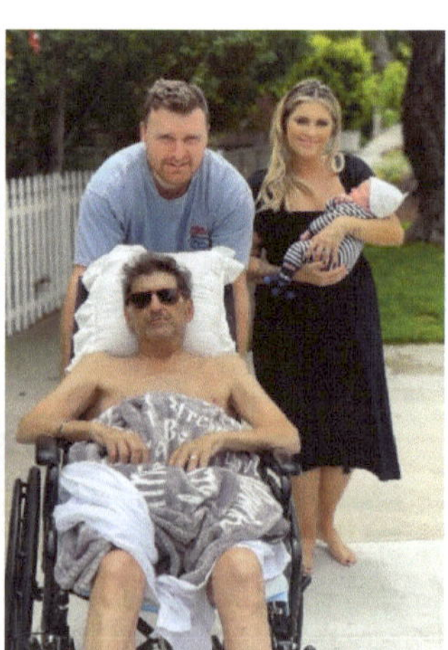

Painful Goodbyes Begin

Grandson Angus's Goodbye

Creating Smiles

The Boys

CHAPTER 3
I HAVE A CONFESSION

One night many years ago, Ken, our Bouviers long since passed, and I strolled in the mild evening, the air thickened by mother Neptune's Pacific Ocean. A block from our home in South Redondo, we happened upon a scene that has since changed my perspective and opened my eyes – but the confession is, that dusky scene took me almost twenty years to fully understand, until a commonality opened my innocent eyes.

This is what we witnessed that foggy night:

We happened upon a private residential garage transformed into a hospital room. Propped up in a state-of-the-art hospital bed, its equipment blinking, I.V. poles standing at attention lay a shrunken figure shrouded in a puddle of pale fluorescent light. This incongruous incomprehensible sight stunted our manners. Our frozen gaze from the sidewalk made its rude intrusive presence known; we had stared for too long, and the garage door abruptly descended – closing in unison with our agape mouths.

I am ashamed to confess my naïveté. I was horrified, astonished by this out-of-place makeshift mini-medical facility.

It is not so much the image that has plagued me through the years but the fact that I did not understand or recognize the very germane reason behind what we witnessed that balmy, salty night.

As painful as it was to see an ill man living in a garage – I now understand. That night I couldn't have imagined that my very own husband would be living out his last days on a less than state-of-the-art Medicare hospital bed in our living room.

I now know not to judge, that in time answers will reveal themselves more clearly, acutely and personally.

On a bright and sunny June day, as I escorted our lead hospice nurse out of the house and down the newly con-structed hospital ramp, I searched for information perhaps not shared in Ken's presence. Rhonda told me in her heavy British accent about an option called 'Death with Dignity'. M.A.I.D., Medical Aid In Dying. It was a transcendental moment. I'm sure a flock of seagulls could have nested in my open mouth wide with incredulity – I wasn't aware this type of death was legal in California. It had never even entered my otherwise preoccupied mind. Instinctually upon hearing this revelation, I vehemently rejected the notion of sharing it with Ken. The thought was too terrifying; I knew he would choose this path. He was all about control. I didn't feel capable of forming the words needed to tell him he had this option, yet deep down in the most sacred part of my soul, I knew what my obligation was. It was Ken's right to explore this option, his option, his choice, and so I did. I wish I could remember how I broached the subject, but I do not. I know it took extreme emotional fortitude.

Ken, as anticipated, was eager to learn more and to 'sign up', as if he was signing up for Tango lessons. This medical choice aligned with his desire for total control. His whole life he chose control, and for the last several months he had been deprived of it.

Together we learned how terminally ill patients under hospice care who have a diagnosis of under six months to live, qualify for M.A.I.D., if approved by the overseeing Hospice Doctor and also approved by the Doctor prescribing the lethal medicine. It is a process requiring physical and cognitive evaluations over a fifteen-day period of time. (This may be changing and shortened pending current legal decisions.) He wanted to start the process immediately. I believe Ken sensed his disease's neurological component was beginning to take hold. He could feel the window of his cognitive abilities closing. I witnessed his mental acuity decline in fragments every day.

Ken's disease, Amyloid, is a sticky, starchy protein that attacks many areas of the body, including the brain. Ken was getting forgetful. He had a hard time using his cell phone, both mentally and physically. He was emotional and weepy. He was struggling, and in order to qualify to 'die with dignity', he had to be cognitively aware of what he was undertaking and physically able to drink the lethal potion without aid. Part one of Ken's process to be qualified to die with dignity: The supervising hospice doctor with Torrance Memorial sat with Ken for almost two hours. It seemed more of a social call than an evaluation. They shared a love of racquetball and knew people in common. But in reality, the good doctor was assessing Ken's mental aptitude. He passed assessment round one. A few more remained, and then the rest was up to Ken.

According to research, a very high percentage of people who obtain the medicine never use it. The dying person simply finds comfort that the medicine is available at their immediate discretion. Another percentage doesn't live long enough to take the medicine. Ken wanted to go out with a bang, not a whimper. He wanted to take the medicine.

CHAPTER 4
CONTROL

Ken chose the date of his death to be August 3, 2021. He wanted to include his best friend. Our adult children felt it too traumatizing to contemplate being present. The Death Doula, a new volunteer position with Torrance Memorial, was helping Ken plan his death path, from who would be present to the atmosphere, music and scent of candles in a similar vein as a Birthing Doula. Sean told Ken that whatever Ken wanted for his death journey, he'd make it happen. The floodgates had been opened.

Ken declared he wanted to have a 'living' memorial like his friend George who had passed some years previously. He wanted a huge party with friends, neighbors and my closest clients. Sean the Doula didn't realize what he signed up for! Ken confused 'death doula' with Party Planner. Ken began giving Sean directions, aka orders in exquisite detail of what he wanted; cocktail height tables with linens, a band, catering from Nate n' Als, very specific invitations, custom T-shirts and MUCH more. Luckily for us, our dear friends Jerry Garbus and

David LeFevre, the talented South Bay restauranteurs came to our aid, or rather Sean's! How I laughed and continue to laugh at this phase of Ken's time in hospice.

This epic living memorial on July 11, 2021, was a wonderful diversion during the planning stages. It occupied most of Ken's waking hours, designing the special order T-shirts, the food, the music, the cocktail height tables and linens. Ken was pretty bossy. Ken's youngest son AJ made the E-vites complete with an amazing photo of Ken in his peak athletic youth – mid catch of a frisbee between his tan legs in mid-air.

The day arrived. July 11, 2021. The garden was set up. I was ready. All the plans were set into motion. Ken had spent ninety-nine percent of his time in his hospital bed, and it was time to put him in his wheelchair. These seldom transfers to his rolling chariot made me very nervous. He had almost no strength to steady himself upright. Our amazing neighbor and dear friend Jeremy used his strength to ease Ken into his rolling throne. Only one small hiccup... Ken suddenly had to use the toilet, which required a military operation. He hadn't sat on his warm Toto Washlet toilet for weeks. He described it like visiting with a dear old friend. The hilarity of the moment added levity to the heavy tension. Finally, Jeremy delivered Ken to his living memorial in our garden.

The living memorial was exactly as Ken visualized it, pastrami, roast beef deli platters from Nate n' Al's lined the kitchen counters (the title of the E-vite was 'Ken's Last Deli Platter'). Amazing desserts from Chef David filled the fridge. Wine, beer and soda spilled out of huge ice-filled tubs. Table cloths fluttered in the warm summer air. The latin band, a gift from dear friend Freddy, played lively music and even managed our song, 'Harvest Moon' by Neal Young. I serenaded Ken with a strong voice filled with emotion. There wasn't a dry eye that day. People came from all corners of LA. The Redondo Beach Fire Department and Fire Chief brought the biggest fire engine with the tallest ladder. The amalgamated gathering of friends, family neighbors posed for a photo testament of love; Ken in the middle smiling broadly from his wheelchair wearing a Balinese sarong, Hawaiian shirt and oxygen cannula, flanked by me, his brother and best pal of sixty years and at least fifty others. It was a precious moment for all. I felt triumphant, basking in the glow of my beloved's exhausted smile.

Ken began to eat more. He was more lively. He wanted to sit on the couch. I chided myself for not thinking of moving him from the bed. He insisted on standing to feel the floor beneath his feet where a few weeks before it would have been impossible. He did it for a brief moment, but I couldn't help but notice that one foot was totally purple and the other not. Sometimes I had to let go. Let go of my fear to let him live, if just for a moment and allow him to die.

My husband, crazy and thoughtful, planned one last mission with a little help from his co-conspirators; our neighbors and dear friends Jeremy and Lisa.

This adventure on July 16, 2021, would be the first time since his arrival home on June 19, 2021, that he would venture out of the house. We were going to El Cayote for lunch, his last wish, or so I thought.

When the day arrived, we needed to load Ken into the medical van. I was overly anxious. Simply getting him out of bed and into the wheelchair, down the ramp to the curb was a military maneuver. Oxygen tank, catheter bag, Floyd, me, Jeremy and his wife Lisa climbed in, squeezed into the van. Ken was in rare form. He was excited and so much his old self. En route, the surprise was foiled. I was told we were only going to lunch. But it became apparent that there was to be a stop before lunch. I instantly knew where we were headed. My husband, he had this planned all along. I was so gullible. He got me every time. He loved surprising me.

We pulled up to my favorite shop in Beverly Hills and the men got out, Jeremy, Floyd and Ken who was still exhausted from the party five days prior. Lisa and I were told to stay in the van and to wait. I was desperately worried; I had separation anxiety. They were locked in the shop for two hours. I hadn't been apart from his side for more than a quick bath over the last weeks, and he always complained that I took too long.

Peeking in the door, I could see Ken weeping, writing notes, bags all around him, his hands clutching tissues. My heart wept at the sight of him, glasses in his hands, wiping the tears as Floyd comforted him. In the video Floyd took, I could see the difficulty he was having breathing; his chest fighting for air. I needed some comforting as Ken had the Platinum American Express in hand, and God only knew what he had charged up! Hell, he knew he wouldn't have to worry about the bill once he died! It was a moment in time that touched all around Ken. Floyd wrote this after the end of the day:

> *An overflowing of thoughts and emotions.*
>
> *I can't exactly describe the feeling that I have never imagined to have witnessed today. The feeling of the excitement, joy, sadness, anxiety, overwhelmed and helplessness, all combined together that have stricken out the very vulnerable part of my heart.*
>
> *Sometime, one day many years ago, I felt a very similar feeling that I wished would never be experienced again, but life, after all, is full of revelations and mystery.*
>
> *One sunny day of July, late morning of Friday, when my patient (Mr. Ken), his wife (Mrs. Alison), son and close friend neighbors went for a planned day-out. Somewhere and nowhere in our heads, having no idea what's going to happen. We headed further away from their home and watched a blue sky and the ocean as our beautiful background. And that moment all I know is, I am going to be a*

spectator of a very thoughtful and sweet husband of Mrs. Alison Clay-Duboff, aside from being his caregiver.

Mr. Ken Duboff was a loving husband, a father of three and a grandfather too, a man who was loved by many of his family, friends and neighbors. Needless to say, he is also a good-looking man at his age. A man who I would say loves to travel good places, a dog lover, has a quite weakness to sumptuous foods, not to mention his fondness for drinks and booze, and loves to explore many different exciting things and a man with a great sense of humor. Sadly and painful as it can be, he was terminally ill and counting his great and final moments with his family and friends, and that only our Creator can tell. Maybe If I would have found and known Ken sooner, I must have enjoyed my work so much better. Maybe, after all, I am imagining how my father would be as much as cool as Ken. Don't get it wrong, I love my father very much and I know he does too but we just don't have our best moments yet as father and son.

Well, I would still call this day as the most cinematic yet romantic kind of event. When one man tried to still act selfless and very loving husband to his wife. I would normally see these things in movies but today I have seen it with my very own eyes how on earth would a man, even at his final remaining days, chose to surprise Mrs. Alison or rather always go for the happiness of his wife. For those who don't believe in love, now is the time to hear it. Alison would even describe their relationship as "We complement each other, I am him and he is me." That they would seek each other's help about a very tiny bit of detail in every situation they needed each other. In other words, codependent.

Goosebumps. Yes, I had many of that today too. Imagine a man in a wheelchair with oxygen circling around in the sunny and busy streets of Rodeo Drive in Beverly Hills, where top-of-the-line and high-priced fashion brands are situated, believe it or not, he did a shopping for her beloved wife. I never saw that coming, I too was very surprised.

Touched down. The door opened for us. And there we were, the vibrant color of Hermes welcomed the three of us while his wife and close friend neighbor waited outside. And no, astonished as his wife was with everything that was going on, she was not allowed to get a glimpse of how Ken would select the finest gifts of all time for his darling, and this is how much he wanted to build the element of ultimate surprise for his dear wife.

My heart melted for them, especially for Ken. I had a pounding heart right there. Even though I felt like being choked, I mustered up my courage not to cry, and still tears shed to the lining and lid of my eyes, and I finally decided to put my shades on before it goes down to my face, so no one can ever notice. They had experienced an amazing life to-gether, and now this happened to them in just a blink of an eye. Their faith has been twisted around from up to their lowest suffering. So don't you dare laugh about this because life is so uncertain, most of the time, it is not fair.

care·giv·er
/ˈkerˌɡivər/
noun. NORTH AMERICAN
a family member or paid helper who regularly looks after a child or a sick, elderly, or disabled person.

But allow me to give you a little deeper meaning into it because being a caregiver is indeed a very challenging job. But what makes it more challenging is the emotional investment you impart to each and every patient you encounter. Yes, now that I have mentioned it. Many would say and advise to not sympathize but rather show empathy. However, easy as it may sound, I can only show true feelings that are genuinely coming out from my heart, and that is my real or true compassion towards them. Some would say many other hideous things, even though they know nothing about what it means and what it takes to be a 'CAREGIVER'. Because by the way, it also means that when you sign up for it, it will also mean that you touch many people's lives. So to speak, let's add up to the qualifications required when looking for a caregiver; the ability to withstand every surprise and different strong emotions you encounter day by day.

The more you give, the more and deeper feeling you get involved in it. The inevitable pain and unimaginable hurt that you could feel to someone that is not even your blood but became part of your life. But are we supposed to give our very best effort and feeling to what we are doing? And so I say, the less effort and feeling we invest, the less passion and sense of fulfillment you feel however makes you less hurt and also makes you feel less of a human too.

I am not saying that I am now an expert in this field because all I know is that I still have a lot to learn. I am still hungry to be educated and equipped with knowledge. I do, and I will always crave for it, to sharpen my blade and gain more wisdom. I acknowledge, too, that I am still far from all of it. All I can say is that I am proud of my job, my current position, my bread and butter. It is decent and most fulfilling job, and I have taken it very seriously. I will give my eveything to it because I care a lot about my patients and would always try to provide love, understanding, support and effort to all of them without any reservations. Never did I imagine that I would somehow land on this profession. So shout out to all caregivers out there. Keep going because you play a very important part of a community or rather in the world that we live in. Cheers and salute to all of you, and put your head up high!

The sole purpose of me writing this piece yet remarkable event is to able to share with you a wonderful and unforgettable story, a story that I have experienced personally. Enclosed with it is the unconditional love for his wife and their romantic and beautiful love story, together with my uncontainable feeling of full and mixed emotions. Above all, to say to all of you that I love and how very proud I am of this profession. Lastly, to be able to share with you a love that is so divine and precious, a love that may **not be so perfect but a love that is so true and real.** ♡

Lunch at El Cayote wasn't what Ken hoped for. He was so emotionally drained and physically depleted he could barely take a sip of water. Ken was amazing. I ache in recollection.

During those last weeks, I tried to fulfill Ken's wishes and desires, his newly shrunken bucket list. Friends came over to say their farewells, family came over to say their heart-wrenching goodbyes. Each goodbye ripped our collective heart from our chests. I could feel Ken's aguish consuming his body. His skin smelled of heartbreak, each farewell consumed our souls with agony.

Time was standing still and speeding forward simultaneously. August 3 was approaching, and secretly I hoped Ken would pass peacefully in his sleep and we wouldn't go through what we were about to go through.

However, in a weird and indescribable way, we actually enjoyed the last few weeks of his life. His eldest son, Scott, wife and the grandkids came to visit and turned the house upside down with youthful glee. Each child laid with Ken, naturally and with young love laced with confusion. My daughter, her husband and their three-week-old baby, my grandson, came to visit. The beauty of those moments will keep me warm with bittersweet emotions for the rest of my life. Reconciliations were made, sad confessions professed. Ken held each one of his grandchildren in his frail, thin arms and whispered goodbyes. Friends came in and out – it was a warm and loving heart-wrenching time. We drank a lot. I was always making cocktail concoctions.

Another night on the couch I put my sentiments into words whilst Ken slept.

I can hear the music's dissonant melody – the music of our love journey, our now life into death excursion. It is akin to an innocent carousel ride at the county fair. Up we glide, inhaling the fresh air, feeling the exhilaration of a weightless tummy borne of love, borne of butterfly wings and knowing glances, the finishing of each other's sentences, that look. Oh, that look.

Abruptly and swiftly as we rose to meet the clouds, the basket bumps its way down earth side, to land on the stark reality we face. We are coming to the end of our A ticket rides.

Time is short, shorter than we ever contemplated imaginable. Ken and I are codependent, and our hearts pump each other's life's blood. Whence forth his ceases, my heart will no longer be whole.

One day on the couch, I gingerly brought up the topic of Ken's obituary. Knowing Ken the way I did, I knew he would get a perverse kick out of co-authoring his own obituary. We worked on it together – odd, but we found laughter in the task. We had much to talk about, but we limited our subsequent discourse to a few unanswerable questions. Most evenings moments of silence laid heavy in the air. Depleted, disheartened and dismayed, we wandered around the souvenirs of our twenty years. Glorious and golden, majestic and mercurial, emblazoned on our collective memory, we shared our combined reflections. We smiled. And that sufficed.

From the depths of a dark, dank well with no visible bottom and no surface light filtering downward, I try to find the courage to scale towards a vision of what my future will look like without Ken. Do I dare ease into a fleeting sideways glance, creep gingerly towards a proximity to the new empty canvas as it advances closer every day? I fleetingly give my mind permission to conjure a charcoal-scratched Ken-less landscape, and suddenly, instantly, I retreat to the soft, sad comfort of his breath. He is here with me now. I grasp his hands in gratitude, following the road map of his skin – each inch I trace by heart.

The still wheels of the walker no longer awaited his

pitter-patter. The pill bottles stand at attention, ready for battle.

Tomorrow is a new day.

I despise myself for moments of self-pity. I remind myself in no uncertain terms of the fear and suffocating sadness Ken must feel, how he must choke on every shallow breath, wondering if his bride will awake to himself no more.

I loathe his pain, his fear, his worry and dread. I want to consume it, devour it, rip and bite it with my teeth yet I softly caress his face, startling the tender shoots of his nerves as he flinches under my touch.

There were moments, little shards of seconds when I allowed myself to luxuriate in forgetfulness and pretend that all seemed right in our world. Our little island universe unto us alone, I would close my eyes and travel through the galaxy of love.

I am you, and you are me. We laugh to each other.

David and I celebrate Ken

Ken's Living Memorial

Father and Son

Last Shopping Spree

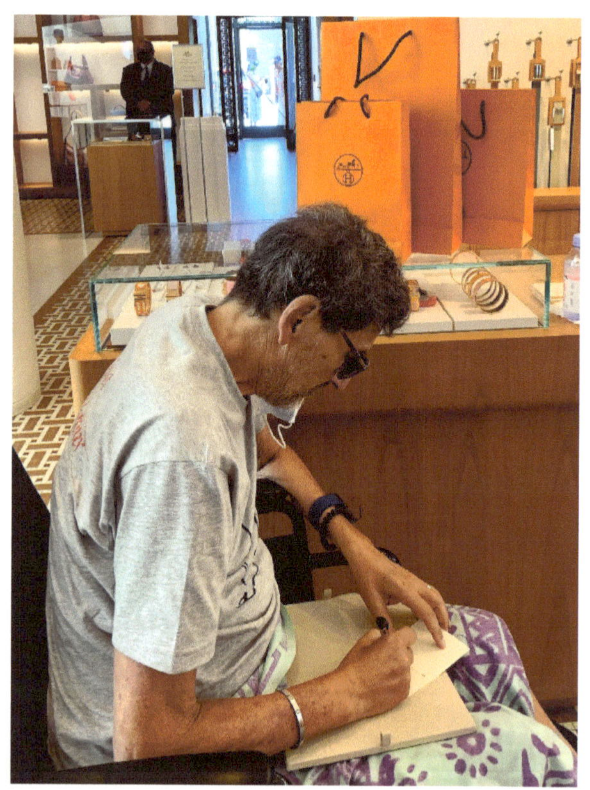

Last Note

CHAPTER 5
LAST OF MANY

I got up and asked my husband what he wanted for his very last breakfast. He requested 'Alison pancakes', strawberry jam (Smuckers) and maple syrup (Log Cabin). Oh, the irony of that request.

Ken was a very precise and detail-oriented person. You could say he was, well, at times, very annoying. He used to boast about taking some weird organizational class that I can't remember. Anyway, Ken managed the pantry. We always had three of everything. One for current use, one to replace and one spare. It was all about the rotation of items to never run out. I, on the other hand, am much less methodical when it comes to such mundane home economics. I have been running out of everything ever since he passed.

And yes, a few days prior, I had used the last of the strawberry jam. Being more of an apricot jam person and attempting to be practical in the light of Ken's future physical absence, I didn't order any more strawberry. Oh, how I regret that decision.

On the last full normal day of Ken's life, he wanted MY pancakes (he would not be allowed to eat the next day), and I didn't have the necessary. I ran out of STRAWBERRY FUCK-ING JAM. How could I have been so thoughtless? It's not like I could have run to the store. It would have been very odd for me to 'dash' out. I hadn't left his side for months. The guilt, self-loathing of not being able to fulfill his last meal request on death row countdown consumed me. It was unthinkable.

That's why Ken wanted Kathy there. Kathy, Ken's friend of fifty years, was the calm needed. Ken had planned her presence in my life. In the moment of my secret angst, she put her hands on my shoulders and reminded me I had two wimpy-looking strawberries in the garden box Ken had built for me months prior, a lifetime ago. Ken didn't eat strawber-ries, so I would have to make 'pretend' Smuckers. I ran out and plucked them, scrawny as they were, washed and muddled them with a tablespoon of Karo syrup. Necessity is indeed the mama of invention. I garnished his hotcakes with my makeshift strawberry jam, swirled maple syrup on top (a nice dose of high fructose corn syrup), served them with love, and he ate them all, never the wiser.

His last lunch I've long forgotten, but his last dinner is fresh in my mind. The amazing Chef David delivered Rib Eye, Jumbo Shrimp Cocktail and more. Ken loved the fact he delivered his meal with flowers, shorts and a big smile.

We spent our last night, August 2nd, in our bed. It seemed only natural, and we managed the logistics. We both wanted it desperately. How long had it been since the last carefree night in our safe haven? How many nights had we clung to one another in the blissful ignorance of twenty years of worry-free nights? Twenty years of nights, twenty years of love-making, of TV watching, twenty years of footsies. But this night was unlike any other. This night would be our last night ever.

I don't know how I heard Ken as his voice was as soft as our beloved milky moonlight, but I heard him whisper, **"hold me,"** and I did. I clung to him as if my hug could reverse time. I held him with a love more profound than I ever thought imaginable. I will always wonder if Ken felt my warm tears streaming down his beautiful back.

Last Breakfast

D DAY, D FOR DEATH, DEPARTURE

August 3, 2021

My nickname was Sunflower

At first light, Ken turned to me with the most beautiful Ken smile. "I made it – I'm still here," he grinned at me on this, his last Tuesday morning – ever. I kissed him.

His face was soft but resolute as he spoke these words, "I control the disease or the disease controls me," he continued with Ken-like panache, "I want to go out with a bang, not a whimper." I honestly believe he willed his body to live so he could end it his way.

The day of Ken's self-scheduled death we had planned a

small gathering consisting of my sister, Ken's brother, Kathy and a few dear friends. Ken amazed me yet again. When the time arrived, he insisted on walking from the bedroom to the living room where the guests would gather. Kathy and I hovered around Ken like moths around a flame whilst he slowly took steps. It took time but he made it, whereas weeks before, he couldn't even sit at the edge of the bed without his bp plummeting. He was my Jesus, walking on water.

The emotionally charged group arrived. We made champagne toasts, emptied the Hibiki from his treasured bottle. He had to restrict the amount of alcohol so the lethal elixir would absorb properly in his gut. How could I tell this man I loved so completely not to enjoy another thimble of Hibiki? Small reflections were shared. There were tears and laughter. Myself, caregiver JoJo and Kathy sang him "Harvest Moon"

Final Goodbyes

per his request. JoJo had practiced for days prior. It's amusing to think that JoJo's singing had initially annoyed him; how things change when staring death in the face.

I honestly believed then and will continue to believe to this day that Ken willed his body to live until his death day, the day he would exit this world with a bang and not a whimper.

Everyone uttered their final goodbyes and departed. Nurse Nick who would mix the potion and oversee the process, Sean the Doula, my sister, JoJo and Kathy and I remained. The dogs paced and panted.

The nurse asked if Ken was ready for the pre anti-nausea

meds. He said he wasn't. I can't imagine what was going through his mind. How could he have been so calm? How did he know when he was ready? I knew that I could never be ready, never. He must have known that as well.

Dr. Death, as I called him, previously gave us a description of this end-of-life process. He told Ken and me it would be the most beautiful passing, peaceful, calm and simply serene. We were told how families often gather around their loved one, they would share tears and laughter. A beautiful ending to a beautiful life, a peaceful and tranquil passing for all. I clung to that.

After the guests had departed and when Ken was ready, he took the anti-nausea medication; he was not allowed to eat after midnight the night before, and his last dinner was supposed to have been light; but it was far from that, and he drank more booze than was recommended. The reasoning behind the restrictions has to do with the body's absorption of the medications, which is in powder form. The more food in the body, the slower the absorption rate. The anti-nausea meds are given one hour before drinking the medicine.

Once the medicine is ingested, the Doctor explained, the patient falls deeply asleep, and within an hour to several hours later, their heart stops, and they pass. Everyone is different, I was told. It could take one hour or up to fifteen hours, but our Dr. thought with the advanced state of Ken's illness, most likely he would pass in one hour, but he reminded me to be prepared for longer, and I was.

I won't go into the financial details of the process to have the right to die with dignity. Let me just state for the record it's not cheap nor covered by insurance. It's ugly to put a price tag on the death of a part of your soul.

Eventually, Ken was ready to move to the next step. We moved to the bedroom, and again he walked under his own steam, on those holocaust skinny legs. He even wanted to have his picture taken in just his undergarments, Kathy and I flanking his sides. I'll never know why he wanted to memorialize such an intimate image or what he'd want me to do with it in the future.

Nurse Nick mixed the lethal potion of Morphine and Lorazepam, which had been locked up in a drawer. It comes in a powder form. Apple juice is added to make the taste more palatable, but there is no masking the sour, bitter, burning taste.

The mixture ends up being a few ounces, and you have to drink it within two minutes, or you fall asleep with the possibility of not finishing the entire dose. Also, the combination of meds is extremely bitter. It is so bitter it burns the throat. I've learned hence that it tastes like ammonia with a shot of bleach, magnified by a few million.

We were told people very often never end up using the medication. It's presence on the night table gives the terminally ill sufficient peace simply to know it was there, available if they wanted it.

It pains me that I don't remember what I said to Ken or what he said to me before he drank this intense concoction. What I do remember is he told me he would try to squeeze my hand if he could. And I, in turn, told him how much I loved him and that we had already said our goodbyes numerous times. I also gave him a final 'out' if he didn't want to follow through and that no one would hold any judgment against him if he chose to die, naturally, eventually.

I wish I could remember and cling to the feeling of our last kiss, but I don't, I can't. I was in a state of auto pilot and extraordinary shock. I don't know how I was able to bravely support him without totally losing it. Perhaps it was because I knew how utterly important his death journey was to him, and if I broke apart, it would make his passing so much harder for his release. I already knew how much and how deeply it pained him to leave me behind and how brave he had to be. I owed it to Ken to see it through with grace and dignity.

After a few small spoons of lemon sorbet to chill his throat, he lifted the cut crystal glass to his lips. He chugged it down in one horrifying gulp. He then uttered his last words on earth, **"that sure did a number on my throat."** I'm so sorry that it hurt him. There's got to be a better way.

The patient has to drink the entire mixture in under two minutes because if you don't, you risk falling asleep without finishing the entire dose. I don't know what would happen or what has happened or if it ever has happened that someone didn't finish it in its entirety. Did they fall asleep before finishing the mixture and become brain dead? Did they pass away anyway just from half of the dose? These are answers I don't have and maybe one day I will seek them out.

Within a few minutes, Ken closed his eyes. At 2 pm, to the utter amazement of all who knew and loved him, Ken permanently put an end to his disease. Then let out what I can only describe as a primordial scream which made me jump out of my soul in terror. Was he in pain? Was he suffering? What was happening? This wasn't forewarned to me. I could sense it sort of freaked out the nurse. Either he or I asked if Ken needed more morphine. I don't remember. It was decided not to be given.

For the next five and a half hours, Ken had what's called agonal breathing, it sounded like horrific gasps for air coming deep from his chest. His chest would rise and fall, and then there were moments of extreme snoring beyond a regular snore. The nurse explained that this was the natural response of the body trying to save itself. I was not forewarned of this either. It was traumatizing, agonizing, unimaginable and unforgettable. I sat up in bed next to him holding his hand, waiting for the squeeze that never came. I was high as a kite on cortisol, heart racing, pulse-pounding. The candle Ken chose burned at the side of the bed. Harvest Moon and his other musical selections meant to send him on his way played in the background. Every god-forsaken minute was like five hundred eons. And yet three hours passed as if in a flash. I'm not totally sure where I was, what astral plane I inhabited during those moments.

Throughout the hours the nurse would take Ken's pulse – he would proclaim that his pulse was striated and that it was slowing, but when I put my head to his chest, his heart was beating soundly into my ear. I was utterly conflicted.

After three or so hours my sister, Kathy and the Doula could hear the noises and decided I needed support. I had to go to the bathroom, I had to catch my breath, I had to cry, I had to somehow take a break if just for a moment. It may seem funny be we ate Thai food on the bed while Ken continued on his death march. I don't remember that but I was told we did.

With the door opened as Kathy, Sean the Doula, and my sister sat on the bed with Ken, I suddenly realized I hadn't let the dogs up on the bed to say their goodbyes. Ken and I had discussed whether the dogs should be on the bed during the entire process, but once the process commenced, I temporarily forgot about the dogs.

Ken was still sitting upright in bed with me to his left, holding his hand. I realized he would want the dogs near him, if only for a moment. I chided myself for not thinking about their relationship.

I was promised by the nurse that Ken had been completely unconscious in a deep, deep coma during those five and a half cruel hours. He was so loud. I was terribly frantic, thinking he would awake, or vomit, or try to speak. I was beside myself with anxiety, fear and nerves. I don't know how I didn't expire along with him. There is a large part of me that wishes I did.

I invited the dogs in. Babu jumped on the bed, sniffed his dad, licked his fingers and then jumped off the bed. I.V., the eldest, took one sniff and curled up next to me. Within moments of the dog's presence, Ken's breathing calmed, slowed, and he passed. He was gone. My Ken was gone.

My sister was worried Ken had not actually passed, she couldn't bear any more suffering, misery for me, but I assured her he was gone, and I lifted up the sheet to show her his skin; it was mottling very quickly upon the cessation of his last breath and his last heartbeat. His skin was soft as silk, as always.

Once he had passed, I removed his wedding ring and put it on my finger, removed his love bracelet and put it on my wrist next to mine, collected his brown prayer bead bracelet from India, and closed his eyes. I don't remember kissing him, but I'm sure I did. The nurse pronounced him dead. I wish I could kiss him yet again. I wish I would have smothered him in kisses; maybe I did but I don't think so. I was being brave. I was being Alison, the Nordic warrior, noble and dignified. In control, taking care of Ken in his death so soon after life. I was still taking care of my husband.

The protocol is to immediately call hospice. The death Doula Sean called hospice, and the nurse came and officially pronounced Ken dead, noted the time of death and called the mortuary. I had already chosen his urn; I had even shown Ken what I had chosen. He wanted to be part of the process, to walk alongside me in my pre-grief, my anticipatory grief.

When the lone slender mortuary employee arrived a few hours later, or maybe it was a bit less, I aided him in wrapping Ken's body in a simple white sheet, moving him to the gurney. In Ken's usual contrarian spirit, his jaw refused to stay closed, and his eyes kept sliding open. *This* was too much for me.

Ken had ordered the dismantling of the wheelchair ramp two days prior to his death, as he didn't want "Alison's home to look like a dead man's house." So I helped the young mortuary man carry the gurney down our front steps and into the van, that was conspicuously not a Hearse for which I was grateful. Surprisingly there was an empty gurney inside the van, and I asked the young man if he had another stop on his way to Ken's final destination. He laughed kindly and said, "No, no, mam, he's my only one tonight."

I shut the double doors of the van and rested my hands on the glass. I bade my husband's physical body goodbye and watched the van until it was no longer in sight. I stood in the street and howled at the moon.

Ken's favorite quote throughout hospice was looping in my mind as I stood alone on the quiet, empty street.

"In the end, we are all just walking each other home."
        – Ram Das

CHAPTER 6
THE CHALICE

Ken taught me one particularly important lesson (of many) shortly before his death. He seemed to know my DNA coding and could read it like a page-turner. We have a matching pair of Baccarat tumblers and one pair of matching Lalique champagne flutes. He knew I would reverently idolize them as they held so many priceless liquid memories. He knew they would never rest upon my lips after he passed. So one day when a dear friend came for a visit, he asked me to serve them both a small finger of Hibiki in our 'special' tumblers. My reaction was said without a word. Ken replied with a naughty grin, "I want you to enjoy these glasses for years to come, so let's destigmatize them now."

On the day of his designated death, I needed a vessel for his prescription. It had to be big enough for several ounces, so I chose a large elegant punch glass of his late mother's. We used to debate which of our mothers it had belonged to, but I let him have that win.

Nurse Nick mixed the powder with apple juice which

didn't disguise the rank bitter flavor or burning sensation. What followed that August afternoon is history, but this punch glass I refuse to be afraid of. I refuse to hide it from my sight, to be fearful of its new symbolism. Instead, I use it daily, with the respect the glass deserves. Ken was able to go out with a bang, his wish granted thanks to the law in California. I shall respect the chalice forever.

Home

Good Bye My Love

CHAPTER 7
RUNNING AWAY
FROM GRIEF

Early on during Hospice, I recognized I needed to enlist Ken's help with tasks, unimportant in the scope of our new life, yet critical to my life ahead without him. I needed him to give verbal authorization on shared credit cards, needed to learn his 'banking systems', needed to figure out his autopay, his bill pay and countless other mundane administrations of life when all I simply wanted was to lay in his arms. That wasn't even possible very often as the hospice bed was small, and his body was excruciatingly tender.

We both knew that once this excruciatingly painful journey was over that I would need to escape, to flee the memories, the gargantuan weight of what I went through, what our home retained, the experience of his illness, of his death, of my frailty.

One day I overheard Ken on speaker phone with American Express Travel, his best friends of travels past. He could barely talk and was sobbing while trying to explain to Amy, the 'travel expert', that he wanted to plan a trip for his wife for after he died. I heard Amy crying, Ken crying, I was crying, and Floyd in the kitchen was trying to stifle his own gasps of heartbreak. It was one of the most painful moments in this personal story of heartbreak.

Ken and Amy were discussing an idea I had divined a few days earlier. The ill-thought-through hare-brained idea was a cruise, I thought it would be the ideal escape. I could stay in my cabin all day or wander the decks. I could have room service or eat at the Captain's table; my choices would be confined to the boundaries of the ship, fewer choices, less thinking. AND, I was hell-bent on crossing the Atlantic. Why? I have no idea. Ken and Amy from American Express discussed a crossing on a small cruise ship of nine hundred passengers with a very nice yet small stateroom. Departure from Spain via Africa and ending up in South America. A twenty-one-day cruise on wide open and very rough seas. I had never taken a cruise before, nor had my husband. Ken listened to Amy, thanked her and hung up. He then painted a very clear picture of me, for me, on the floor, terrified and vomiting and grieving for twenty-one days. He was so wise. The Atlantic grief crossing of mine was nixed, and Sweden was born.

Ken suggested Paris, after all, it was our favorite city and my second home, but I wasn't ready to imbue that sort of sadness so close to the emotional trauma of his death. Like a flash from the Northern Lights, I decided Sweden was the place to go, into the loving arms of our dear friends whose own love paralleled ours in intensity and depth.

Ken had accumulated about a zillion points, so I was able to book a business class round trip ticket on Air France to Stockholm. I lived in Stockholm some thirty-plus years prior and had not returned since; Ken and I were always invited to the archipelago summer cottage of our dear friends, we just never made it. So it was set.

I knew at some time I had to be a big grown-up widow, and that meant staying by myself, if even for a few nights. After Ken's death and up to the day of my departure, I had 'widow minders', friends and family sleeping at the house. I wasn't alone. I didn't want to be alone then, and I needed this trip **to be able to** be alone. I needed my escape. I focused on nothing else after Ken's death. My trip was all organized, but I had to make sure the dogs and my home would be okay.

We had never had success having someone stay at our house to mind the dogs the way we wanted. But the heavens aligned, and my sister's former student, a filmmaker, was able to house sit, and Bouvier sit. This was a huge leap of faith. At least if it had all gone South, Ken couldn't tell me, "I told you so."

My house sitters and now friends Jonathan and Allison were total dears, but they were cat people. I had to be trusting and let go. Trusting is a gift. And that gift keeps on giving.

All was in order, vaccine documents for the dogs and PCR negative tests for me, passport, Global Entry and I was off.

As I waved goodbye to my dear friend and pillar of support, Gail, at security, I definitely didn't expect that the next time I'd be at LAX, Gail and I would be departing for Paris together.

CHAPTER 8
SWEDEN

Fully alone and with my thoughts, as I walked towards my gate through a neon blue tunnel, it made me think of Ken's passage from this world to the next. At the end of this long blue-tinged hallway, I saw a poster with a brilliant sun setting on an ocean which I guessed was the Pacific Ocean. This walk to my gate seemed inexorably long, and as I walked, I wondered what my future path would be – what would the reason for my life be next – what would I be, who would I be –all these questions washed over me with doubt and fear. But I walked with purpose, dressed for flying, not in sweats and tennis shoes but in heels and make-up. I've always had this notion when flying, you should look chic. I'm old school, and I like it that way. Some habits are hard to break.

Finally, sitting in my business class pod, I introduced myself to the purser; I wanted her to know that if I lost it, she'd know I was a woman bereaved. And true to my inkling as the big silver bird throttled down the runway, as I watched my California coastline disappear into the clouds, I suddenly and urgently had an overpowering need to go home. I sobbed. I sobbed some more. Eventually, the purser came to my side. Good thing I had warned her. I didn't think I'd need her so soon, and this sobbing fit surprised me. I desperately wanted to go, to leave the last months in the past. This departure of mine was ambitious so soon after Ken's death. Letting go is never easy. The Swedish purser held me, kissed me and told me everything would someday be okay. I will never ever forget that warm-hearted woman. I feel I owe her my sanity.

A few glasses of champagne, a couple of movies and a nice dinner served on a linen tablecloth was a wonderful antidote. Ken diligently accumulated these points. He never imagined that I'd be using them without him.

After a few hours of deep Ambien-induced sleep, I arrived in Stockholm feeling fresh and ready for this first solo overseas voyage in twenty years. I had survived the first night away from home across the ocean's expanse. I had made it. When you think you can't accomplish the seemingly impossible, you will surprise yourself.

As I made my way out of security, I saw our dear loving friends waving at me. They scooped me up in their arms, wiped my tears, and we were off to The Grand Hotel, Stockholm.

CHAPTER 9
NEW DAY

It was my first day, my rebirth since Ken died. I was out in the world in a foreign country, wandering without any specific destination, direction or plan. The seven days preceding my arrival in Sweden were consumed with post-death administration that swallowed me whole. I was ready for a break.

Bjorn and Kat, my hosts, were newly engaged (a residual effect of Ken's passing, ie, life is too short to wait for things) and were off to celebrate with family. I felt perfectly capable of exploring Stockholm without Ken, even if he wasn't at my side discovering the golden city with me.

I had lived in Stockholm for a year some thirty years past, but I recognized nothing of the City. I was totally turned around. Stockholm and its ancient cobblestones were a total stranger to me. Grief can coat your memories until obliterated or accentuate the really good ones. If you roll with the recollections, you can actually choose which memories you'd like to re-experience.

Five minutes into my solo foray, I chided death. Widow

Fog or Widow Brain is a veritable condition, and I was deep in the throes of it. Ken had only been gone seven days. I was still in shock. Unwittingly, I stepped directly in front of a very large bus to the gasps of people behind me. I didn't fly all this way to die on the streets of Stockholm. I made a mental note. I needed to be extra cautious.

Five minutes after my near-death experience with the bus, I made my first purchase for our grandson Angus. Ken would have been surprised it took me that long. I bought him a little Nordic Warrior onesie. The memory of Angus's newborn face resting on Ken's chest will remain with me forever. Shopping is a wonderful balm to sadness. Retail therapy, I love you.

As I wandered feeling somewhat carefree, I caught my reflection in a shop window. I looked as if I had aged a hundred years since Ken's passing. The power of grief nudged gravity southbound to wreak havoc on my face. Facials and creams didn't convince my skin to brighten. My face was unconvinced about this new life.

It was impossible to ignore the fact that Ken was not waiting for me at the hotel, he was not waiting for me at a cafe. But I was acutely aware Ken wanted me to continue tasting life, as I strolled through the maze of tiny little pedestrian streets.

I made that my intention. I headed straight for Saluhallen, an indoor market with small restaurants and cafes. I plonked myself at the counter of a shellfish cafe and devoured Swedish whitefish caviar and champagne. I'm sure I radiated solitude as I sat there alone, watching the world carry on as if nothing had changed for anyone except me. The somber reality of who was missing at that counter was palpable. Not a surprise since Ken was my heart's second chamber.

But thanks to Ken, I enjoyed every bite. Thank you for the encouragement to keep tasting life. Thank you, Ken.

I did not feel lonely but very much alone. I thought I had

to engage in battle against grief, and I was determined to be the victor. Grief was my mortal enemy and a fearsome adversary. It would be a slow learning curve to come to the realization I had to embrace grief, not fight it.

As I continued my solo strolling tour of Stockholm, I passed women older and younger than myself, and I wondered, were they widows too? Had they lost someone they once loved with a burning passion?

I stopped to admire an assortment of hanging salamis at an old-fashioned butcher shop and smiled. Ken would have loved it. It was a bittersweet salty moment in a sea of bittersweetness. My emotions were like rolling swells, waves with interludes of calm. In the very early days of grief, you need to savor those moments; they come and surprise you out of numbness.

Watching lovers embracing made me smile, filled my heart. I know some who suffer the loss of a spouse or partner can't connect with the joy they witness. Again, I know I was lucky even though I was an observer of life. But I longed to be a participant.

Running away after the loss of a spouse is an adventure in itself. A litmus test of survival in the big world of singledom. But if I could survive, so could you.

As I found myself alone in Stockholm on the twentieth anniversary of the day Ken and I met, my reflex was to order room service, watch TV get drunk and cry. But I could hear Ken giving me an earful, insisting I shake off the urge to cloister up in sadness and instead dress up and dine out. And that's what I did. I didn't want to upset the sprit of my dead husband! I put on my best dress, a flowing black linen number we bought in Bali the year before, fixed my make-up, chose specific jewelry Ken had given me before his death and had dinner in the finest fish restaurant in Stockholm. More champagne, why not, more caviar, why not, and I rolled out of there satiated, tipsy and feeling very proud of myself. Philip, the hotel's doorman, whisked me up in the open-air electric golf cart, and he gave me a quick tour of the city by night. I let my legs stretch out to feel the cool summer air, and again I found a smile.

The next day, my last in the city, I luxuriated at the hotel spa for a swim in the grotto pool. It was dark and lit with shimmering candles, the water the temperature of my skin. It was curative and very sensuous. I wanted to live forever in that water.

The hotel also had a room with an experiential auditory experience where you sit in a wooden chair, close your eyes, and gong/chimes would ring at specific intervals. It was supposed to calm and purge negative energy. I tried it twice. I think they are on to something.

It was time to join my friends and commence part two of my Swedish escape. I boarded a charming old ferry, direction deep into the archipelago where Bjorn and Kat were waiting.

On board, I met two most amazing gentlemen from Berlin, we all sat on deck with the wind in our hair. They bought me a little bottle of rose (I guess it looked like I needed it), chatted endlessly, and they made the two hours fly by until a slim, fast speed boat pulled up alongside the ferry with Bjorn and Kat waving like lunatics. It was a classic moment I'll never forget. I bade goodbye to my Berliners and renewed a commitment to making new friends along the way, just like Ken and I always did.

I climbed aboard Bjorn and Kat's boat, one of the fastest in the archipelago, and we motored out on deep emerald waters, passing pristine pines and hidden mansions. We turned a corner and alighted upon a tiny harbor where we enjoyed a typical Swedish lunch on a tiny island. We caught up on my adventures in Stockholm, and I drank beer where a few tears had found refuge. We maneuvered the boat out of the sand bar and into the green water. We zipped past doll-like red wooden houses, vast rock formations. The sky was pure Swedish blue, the air brackish like the water, and we navigated down smaller and smaller waterways. Bjorn said I'd easily recognize their summer house; I was suspect as I'd never been there before, but as we rounded the bend I saw a huge flagpole flying the biggest American Flag. Of course I sobbed, but for once, with joy.

My time at their summer home was light, happy and fulfilling. I could talk about Ken without reservations for as long as I wanted, and they did as well. We ate, drank and walked. I even jumped in the water with a half wetsuit – it was cold. Bjorn and Kat had naked morning swims every day; those Swedes, don't know how they do it. Again, you will find yourself being surprised by the things you can do, and stupefied by those you cannot.

The Symbolism was Profound.

My restorative sojourn in the deep green Swedish archipelago drew to a close. I loved it there and could envision myself living amongst the peaceful space between water and land. The tall water reeds bent and swayed, waving goodbye. I lowered the American Flag with reverence in parallel that all good things must come to an end.

I pondered this. Why did it have to end so prematurely? We hadn't lived out our full life together.

I lost Ken on a bright Tuesday in August. His whereabouts unknown, but his permanent residence resides in my heart. I cried hard for the physical.

CHAPTER 10
ACROSS MANY PONDS

My journey across the water far away to the land of Sweden's Vikings was curative and healing. There were happy, joyful, sad and surprising moments tossed together like a green salad with a dressing of salty tears and a heavy heart.

I knew an unknown beginning approached as I inched closer to the home Ken and I built, designed and enjoyed for five years before his achingly permanent departure. As Bjorn and Kat waved goodbye, I knew I was a tiny sailboat set to sea upon calm waters yet knowing there would be storms ahead, large swells of emotion, but at least I was on my way, on my way home.

I left behind a delusional, escapism fantasy trip. The affront of coming home hit me hard and strong in the face. Not by the dogs that licked and knocked me over, but by breathing in the essence of our magical space, our home where Ken exhaled his final soft sigh.

I was forcefully obliged to live a new norm. I'd traveled home racing backwards around the globe. If only life could also go backwards.

I had slept without my other half for seemingly an eternity. I have reached for his hand, my toes longing to entwine with his many a night. Ken inhabited the softest skin, like silk, up to his end. His skin was otherworldly soft.

Perhaps one day I will run out of these tears devoted to Ken.

HOME

My house, uh our house, no my house – whatever – where I live is so pretty, bright and perfect. Ken and I made it that way. But the graceful orchids all around the house were a reminder of the uncharted waters of my new life. I felt so totally alone. Somber and still.

Jet lag plagued me. Up at 5 am and the morning kicked off with a smile. I planted flower seeds from across the pond, played with the pups, did dishes and then dove headfirst into continuing post-death administration. It devoured my life force. The house was so quiet. Even when the dogs barked loud enough to be heard in the next county, it felt so silent.

2 pm, and I stared at the floor, too weary to move away from Babu's famous Bouvier flatulence.

Eventually, we three, me and the two pups, would get our collective acts together. I felt their sadness. I wish I could have offered them more of me. I was tired. My bones were weary. There is good weary, the deep total cellular exhaustion that comes with jet lag; in a way it's beautiful, but you know grief's fatigue is a debilitating curse. You just have to lean into it.

There's no point fighting a fight you will lose.

Grief is also like diarrhea. It sneaks up on you without warning, and it hurts.

CHAPTER 11
MENTAL INSTITUTION WITH A SIDE OF SPA

I still needed a healing place to run away to. I checked out The Golden Door and checked in for a four-day wellness retreat. I had barely spent any time at home since returning, but The Golden Door beckoned to me.

The Golden Door answered, healed and led me to this moment.

As I sit upon crossed knees in reverence to the Japanese shrine in front of me, two months have cumulated since Ken flew away from his and my physical life. For once, phrases, words, syllables are stuck in my throat. I beseech the words to temper my sadness, to expel the sorrow and longing.

Ken came to me last night in a dream as real as the sting of a hornet.

CHAPTER 12
OH NO, MY BIRTHDAY

The day of my birth always enticed Ken to spoil me rotten; I'm not entirely sure who enjoyed these celebrations more, Ken or me. I tried to write down where and how we celebrated for the last twenty years. I didn't get very far because I couldn't get past my surprise fiftieth in Paris.

Ken planned my big fifty for a year. From the moment he woke me the day we left Redondo Beach, the destination was a total surprise. Everyone was in on it; everyone knew the plans. I, however, was totally in the dark. Our driver to the airport held a placard 'I'm Mute'. I didn't know if we were going to Napa, New York or New Delhi. I never expected 'Paris'.

Ken was a master travel planner. It was almost his full-time job. I made the money, and he spent it; he loved it that way and me too.

We shopped for the perfect Little Black Dress; he loved to watch me try on dresses while he observed from a comfortable seat with a glass of something. I would twirl and curtsey and spin, delighting him. The salespeople were always touched by our deep love, obvious affection and, well, just the way we were. ***We stirred people***. We left them with a palpable glow, our love reflected and absorbed by those around us.

Paris was sheer magic, except for the unexpected week he spent in the American Hospital, suffering from an unknown illness with me at his side. We came home without answers, but with a six-week-old puppy. We were nuts.

Yet This year, my fifty-eighth birthday, without Ken was impossible to fathom. In the end it included a car wash (big whoop), a mani-pedi (nice) and then a dinner with a small mismatched group of two friends at my favorite restaurant, The Arthur J in Manhattan Beach, where three years before the same celebration took place and was a lot more joyous. This year I dressed up, smiled, ingurgitated a few oysters and blew out the fucking candles. Birthday over and done.

CHAPTER 13
TSUNAMI WARNING

Purging. I've read this is a very common activity of the newly bereaved. *His* Clothes, *his* books, *his* postcards, letters (mine). Frenetic, manic energy fuels this shedding, this reorganization of a new life. Standing in the reflection of who I now was, honoring who I would become whilst craving who I used to be, who **we** used to be. I was now half of two and it stung, hot and salty on my cheeks. It rendered me sweaty. I was racing ahead of an emotional tsunami. My life's mathematics had been altered, and I was never very good at math.

Trying to avoid the undertow of loss is normal but not beneficial. In the evenings I would sit in Ken's chair acutely aware of my own solo presence, sitting steeped in silence except for the grandfather clock's penetrating gong or one of the dogs' very audible farts. Ken treasured his clock, not the farts. He would polish its' warm oak, lubricate its mechanisms. I used to be afraid of this grand timepiece.

One day during hospice, when his clock stopped, I attempted to dupe time and race the dial forwards due to my impatience. The clock jammed up; froze at 2:20 pm. Ken raged furiously from his hospital bed. In no uncertain terms, I was told I was never allowed to touch his clock until after he died. Some days later, driven by the whimsical nature of his emotions, he insisted I fix the clock before he died. Therein was an urgency that could not be denied. He wanted to hear the ticking, the gongs he loved, on the half and the hour. I spent days begging the Internet to yield a remedy. I knew Google held the answers. The crotchety old timepiece finally yielded, and I reversed time back into its proper dimension. How I wished I could have done the same for my dying husband. At the time the metaphor escaped me. But not now.

In my husband's final days, he told me several times he would 'hang out' behind the Grandfather clock once he was gone, so I, in turn, decided to add my own little dash of humor. I illuminated the Grandfather clock from behind with a bright red nightlight. I keep waiting to cross paths with Ken when I adjust the weights, but it hasn't happened yet.

Ken was gone. My birthday came and went, but the wrenching in my gut, the weak beat in my heart, the never-ceasing questions, the dread, the grief stayed firmly implanted upon my whole being. No point in fighting it. It's part and parcel of the process. Who made these rules anyway.

Moving through this grief is like being suffocated by
marshmallows flavored with vile, bitter bile.
Time is slow yet fast, thick and thin.

CHAPTER 14
PARIS

I had been bravely soldiering on for three months since Ken's death, moving forward through piles of post-death administration, unyielding tasks of absurdness, feeling proud and accomplished. I had made small changes to my inner sanctum, melting a wax seal over the new version of my life. In a fit of pique or vision, I had all the trees and shrubs literally yanked out by the roots in the front of what was 'our home' and replaced them with flowers. Ken would have been irate. I emptied the garage of all of Ken's treasures, old Life Magazines, LPs that were only worth something to Ken. Ken would be irate. I had a redwood deck installed in our rear garden. I was a woman in control, and for that, Ken would have been happy. I'm not sure he'd approve of the bright orange accent wall in the office or the iron ore black accent wall in the dining room, but they make me very happy.

Then Paris happened, and my heart cracked open.

My spirit had been protected by emotional scar tissue and a shroud of shock. But when my pal Gail invited me to Paris, I felt empowered to join her, and we decided to venture forth together to the City of Lights; a girl's trip with frills and delicious possibilities. We were ebullient; Paris was all that and more. The days, the nights. I smiled, I gave Gail the Ken tour of Paris. My social postings bore witness to my joy, and my friends felt equal joy as they scrolled through my smiling posts and commented on how happy they were to see me smile anew.

It's amazing what anxiety can do to a fragile raw soul. Like fire on ether, the French simply had to go on strike the day of our departure. The American Embassy alerted the day before, advising how security would be disrupted, flights delayed, and then our collective panic ensued.

Back in September, in my shroud of shock, I had mis-guidedly booked our tickets on two separate bookings using the points that Ken so deftly accumulated. LA-London, London-Paris, Paris-London, London-LA. But without his travel savoir-faire, I had basically screwed the pooch. At 11 pm the night before we departed from Paris, scant hours after receiving the alert, I realized that Gail was right all along. The yesteryear of travel was no more, and the fact we had two separate flight locators meant we could have zero recourse if we missed our flight to London.

Gail and I brainstormed, thought out every possibility, every potential avenue to overcome the French's desire to disrupt from driving to London to catch our flight to LAX, to taking the Eurostar, or anything else that would get us home. We pattered downstairs in our robes and slippers to enlist the help of the concierge or anyone who would listen to our story of woe. We were stuck in the new world of Covid and the ancient history of 'la greve' in France.

Gail could sense my anxiety getting the upper hand over my sanity. This was only the beginning of our harrowing adventure.

We decided that if we arrived at Charles De Gaulle Airport early enough, we'd clear customs and make our flight with a micro dash of spare time. But due to my major misstep in planning, we couldn't check our bags all the way to LA, we would have to collect the heavy bastards and go through customs at Heathrow and check-in again to connect to our British Airways flight home.

Our outbound flight to London on Air France was delayed due to the strike. What we had not factored in was Air France waiting for every single delayed passenger. Gail and I watched the clock. The purser brainstormed with us. He moved us to First Class so we could be the first off the plane. We had a very small chance to make it.

Time can be a friend or an enemy. We rushed (an understatement) from point A to point B, only to wait and rush again. Thanks to the repercussions of 9/11 coupled with the global pandemic, traveling became a Herculean task of almost insurmountable proportions.

We engaged the aid of the most wonderful porter, Michael, who vowed to not leave our sides till we got to the last stop. He grabbed our bags and sprinted, leaving us two beleaguered mature women pathetically trying to keep up. Then the terminal train was broken, so we had to navigate to the Tube, all the while Michael at the helm like a marathon runner. I could hear Gail's boot heals tapping frantically behind me. There was NO time to spare. Dripping in sweat, we ran and ran for miles through multiple terminals, up and down escalators, on and off trams and moving sidewalks. He weaved through the crowds shouting polite excuses. Then Michael had gotten us as far as he could. Without him, we would have been totally lost. He told us he loved us and sent us on our way, praying to Allah the two sweaty Americans would make their flight.

THEN at the next security point to check into our next

flight, there was a last straw issue of our liquids and gels. Gail and I had purposely packed all of those items in our 'to be checked' bags, but that option long had disappeared. While precious seconds were running out, our bags got flagged with our liquids and gels, and we had to go through further security scrutiny. Makeup got tossed, and my beast of a suitcase had to be opened, and worse, to be closed again. With oppressive time constraints bearing down upon us and with my arthritic fingers, I could not open the tiny combination numbers on the lock. Every millisecond lost was one step closer to failure. Finally liberated from the locks, security searched for all the liquids. A bomb residue detecting device swiped the inside of my bag, its contents strewn in every direction. And then, the 'coup de gras', closing the belly of the beast with all eyes bearing down upon me. The pressure was unimaginable. My fingers worked the locks to no avail. Over and over, I tried in vain as Gail, in late-stage palpitations, watched and as security and I attempted squeezing my bag together. One lock bolted, and clothes peeking out of the sides of my case, we ran again, yelling at everyone in our path. Gail almost took out a pilot and young child. I weaved and bobbed through the throngs of travelers. The distance was unimaginable. We had one last tram with two unbearably long stops. More running and waving our arms as we pushed our roller bags, me wrapped in two sweaters, a vest and coat on the precipice of collapse. We had just one more elevator to reach our gate, of which we couldn't recall the number. The lift was filled with amazingly receptive British Airways crew, and they became our last hope for success. As Gail and I ran blindly out of the lift in the wrong direction, they yelled with loud voices and frantic waves that we were going 'the wrong way'. About face and one more lap to the gate with less than forty-five seconds before the doors closed. We arrived, boarding passes limp and passport at the ready. Once my boarding pass was scanned, I crumbled into a wave of sobs that wracked my body and took my breath away. The gate crew was stunned at my meltdown and ushered us forward toward our aircraft awaiting us with welcoming wings.

Even safely ensconced in my pod, I couldn't stop wailing. My heart cracked open, and all the tears and pain came spilling out. I was truly inconsolable. We made it, Gail proclaimed victoriously, yet I was entering a new phase of grief. This was going to be the beginning of a new heartbreak, new pain, a clearer vision of my loss, of Ken's loss, of our children and grandchildren's loss. Of our doggie's heartbreak too. Gail fell instantly asleep. I continued to weep.

I guess I had it coming. This voyage through grief will surprise me at every turn and will reveal itself in ways I cannot yet imagine. But as I wrote this with a glass of champagne and a salty face, I was going home.

I often wonder what the next years have in store for me. Instead of a sharp pain in the heart, I'm surprised by the little tingle of curiosity.

Paris

CHAPTER 15
DOTS ON THE CALENDAR

Who invented holidays anyway. They are moments in time captured and crystalized on the calendar to remind those who have suffered great loss that their pain hurts exponentially more on certain dates more than others.

I was not as tough as I conjured myself to be during the first holiday season since Ken's departure. It hit me like a ton of raw turkeys; slimy, putrid and impossible to escape. I tried song, I tried an art project, I tried a walk, and eventually, I resorted to Champagne. It was a very long day of nothing in particular until I would wander over to my neighbors to feast with their families. Ken and I avoided family Thanksgivings like the plague. Why did this first Thanksgiving feel so unforgiving? I guess because it was our holiday of rebellion. We would run away from our families; our dirty little escape, yet there was no escape for me this year.

All day I felt like I was waiting for something. Waiting for something to happen or shift or explode or implode. Scant days away from the four-month dreaded anniversary of the death of my lover and my playmate, I had already shifted. I felt naked in my grief, exposed and much more aware of his absence.

The Champagne was cool and fizzy on my tongue. The dogs eyed me suspiciously. I'll never know why on earth they stared at me like that.

This was my new life, the life of firsts without Ken. The awkward time between Thanksgiving and Christmas, toss in a little bit of Hanukkah. What to do with the times in between? 4:30 dinner by the fire, lit candles, Netflix, dogs snoring, wine glass shimmering in the fire's glow. Sounds romantic.

Where do I go from here? Do I know? Do I just go day by day by day by day? I bought a Christmas tree.

I wrapped presents the next morning, staring at Christmas ornaments with eyes half mast, My husband's urn adorned with a Santa hat, Hanukkah hat, prayer beads, Japanese mini pagoda, eternal roses, the season's first acorns harvested on an early morning walk with the pups. I felt like I was suspended in this time and space; it was quite unreal, surreal. Yet the edges were soft and warm.

The future loomed heavily pregnant with mystery as if suspended from the ceiling.

I'm always busy – social engagements, work engagements, animal engagements, yet am I fully engaged? It's the time in between now and the far away tomorrow that defies figuring out. Show me someone who can, and I have a bridge in Brooklyn I can sell you for cheap.

My written words have always been seeds of comfort. They sprout tender shoots of soothing creativity. Such an odd form of therapy, but it quells the tumult inside me. Mere months shy of losing the love of one's life, take what solace you can and wrap yourself up in forgiveness.

CHAPTER 16
FRIENDS AND FOES

People can surprise the hell out of you when you lose a spouse. Maybe they feel the loss is contagious or fear the newly single person could become a threat or adversary. Or perhaps simply some were not true friends in the first place; more of a collaboration of couples who enjoyed being a group who in the face of tragedy become a lesser version of the word 'Friend'.

It astonishes me the way old friends drop away, like dead petals from a flower. I presumed friendships move through the natural course of life, and then new friends blossom on the vine, and I tried to segway myself through these transitions. Yet still, to discover the true nature of someone who once was a close friend and via tragedy turns is toxic. Choices have to be made. There is no place in a heart full of grief for toxic people. Expel them like a big ripe zit.

Grief, pernicious, profound, ambiguous and anticipatory. They all have their moments in the darkness, but anticipatory grief eats you alive every day. The cortisol flows with abandon, tension fills every breath in anticipation of the grief that's yet to come. Like an avalanche in slow motion, you know it's coming, it's going to devour you, suck up all your air and your light, packing you tightly in a frigid unwanted embrace.

When you are moving through grief, it's a time for self-kindness and self-care, not embarking on an epic car trip alone in winter. Even in California, the sunshine state.

I drove up Highway 5 in my new all-electric Audi E-Tron filled with gifts, hopes and my two dogs to spend the holidays with my daughter, son-in-law and baby grandson. The weather was ferocious for California. Charging stations were not uniform or easy to find, even though I had it all mapped out. My mildly arthritic hands made plugging and unplugging the cables a challenge. Rain and wind make for uncomfortable bedfellows. For someone who was so tender and depleted, I think I managed well through tears, a tad of laughter and a lot of anguish. But I made it to Sonoma in one tattered piece.

My daughter and I were overzealous in our planning such an extended stay for me, but Christmas was very special to us; we dreamt not of sugar plums dancing in our heads but binge-watching Netflix and cooking, outdoor hikes and lots of grandma time. In the end, just a few of many days were perfect. We did cook, we did watch a bit of TV, and I had grandma time. The six dogs, one cat, one pig and one goat survived.

The drive back home already felt different. Not in a good or bad way, but again something had shifted. This time I came home to an empty house, no family, no dog/house sitters. This time I felt more directionless even though I had projects and Real Estate business. I ate more, drank more and shopped more. Retail therapy – it's a fine line to walk. Weekly co-pays for therapy would be more cost-effective and beneficial, but shopping has always been my drug of choice.

The Holidays on the Calendar Kept Coming.

New Year's Eve was never a grand celebration for us, we

had our annual program; pizza in bed with a great bottle of champagne. I fully intended on continuing the tradition until I didn't. On the spur of the moment I was cooking for six dear friends. Home-made naan bread (thank you, TikTok) topped with creme fraiche, dill and caviar, beef tenderloin on a bed of beluga black lentils. We were a fun group of friends, some Ken knew, and some Ken will never know. I love through food. He was missed, but he would have been asleep.

CHAPTER 17
A NEW YEAR

Our nineteen Year Wedding Anniversary is January 2nd. I had no plan and wasn't feeling particularly sad or depressed. I was, however, apprehensive about potential feelings, anticipatory sadness. Perhaps I was trying to fool myself into a state of being, one not natural to my situation.

As per my usual, I wrote. I wrote to share with those who warmly received my written sentiments. Many have felt the same emotions of loss but couldn't find the combination of words to express it themselves. These unknowns, strangers in the flesh to me, were grateful for my vulnerability.

"Nineteen years ago today, we stood on the pristine white sand of a tiny little island in the Bahamas with our two daughters and the mayor of the Abaco islands as our only witnesses. We made our vows and became legally bound. It was beautiful, profound and the best day of our lives. But later, when that epic photo was taken of us smooching on the sand, what you can't see was... SAND FLEAS! So behind every story lurks yet another. I'm sharing some other pics of our amazing journey.

19 Years Ago

Last year we had shellfish from Fishing With Dynamite – a beyond generous gift from the owners. Ken could barely eat, and his breath was heavy or light or a little bit of both. We had champagne and made as merry as his body would allow. We didn't know then that within seven months, it would all be over, forever.

What do I know on this day? I know Ken is free of suffering, and for that, I raised my glass tonight.

Ken, I miss you

Ken, I love you

Happy Anniversary wherever you are.

In the end, I had a plan for our anniversary. I was invited to dinner with Ken's dear paddle tennis partner Chris and his wife Joyce, my paddle tennis partner. Chris had walked the walk with Ken during his illness pre- and post-diagnosis, steadfast always. He called Ken every day without fail, came to visit as often as he could. Chris was a devoted friend, and on this night we lifted our glass to Ken. We all missed him.

Ken gave so much to so many, not only by being his generous hilarious self, but by life lessons. I'm not sure he realized the impact his life and his death had on people around him. He made more grown men cry than I'd care to ever witness again. He taught bravery, resilience and a fighting spirit – he didn't want to go. He didn't want to leave me, and of course, nor did I want that.

Ken taught people how to live, how to devour life with mouth dripping life's experiences, sloppy, messy and delicious. He wanted it all, to consume as much joyous adventure, loving companionship and vibrant, intimate love as he could, every day, every moment. We, those left in the foamy wake of loss, need to immerse our sadness into the joyous memories until the gritty sadness of the exercise becomes fluid, like waterskiing on glass.

Happy Last Anniversary My Love

20 Years of Smiles

CHAPTER 18
THE NEXT CHAPTERS

And here I am, months since Ken departed this life on his own terms.

I have traveled thousands of linear and emotional miles to arrive at this junction. I have shed reservoirs of tears, experienced moments of laughter, interludes of contentment, self-introspection and self-realization. I've gained new friends and shed old ones. I am cultivating my new self, and she will be okay. I am committed to moving through the grief and not running from it. I have chosen to push towards life into the unpredictable terrifying blank page that awaits.

When you think you can't, you can.

When you think you won't, you will.

And it's never, EVER over until you decide to turn the page.

ACKNOWLEDGEMENTS

Special heartfelt thanks to The Mayo Clinic Hematology Department, Torrance Memorial Hospice Team, and California for legalizing "Death with Dignity."

Love and gratitude to my sister Lisa who guided me through my first rodeo of loss in 2000, JoJo, Floyd, Kathi and Kathy, Nancy, Gail, Gil, Joan, Lisa and Jeremy, Julie, David LeFevre, Jerry Garbus, Jonas, the Redondo Beach Fire Department; I don't know what I would have done without your caring support.

Deep love to Babu and I.V. whose prescient hairy canine affection made my nights and days bearable.

Sincere indebtedness the legions of caring humans too numerous to acknowledge here, dearest friends across the globe, family near and far, my amazing neighbors, and so many strangers who have guided me along this dark path towards my next bright chapter.

To all those who have experienced loss, my heart holds yours with tenderness.

ABOUT ATMOSPHERE PRESS

Atmosphere Press is an independent, full-service publisher for excellent books in all genres and for all audiences. Learn more about what we do at atmospherepress.com.

We encourage you to check out some of Atmosphere's latest releases, which are available at Amazon.com and via order from your local bookstore:

The Great Unfixables, by Neil Taylor

Soused at the Manor House, by Brian Crawford

Portal or Hole: Meditations on Art, Religion, Race And The Pandemic, by Pamela M. Connell

A Walk Through the Wilderness, by Dan Conger

The House at 104: Memoir of a Childhood, by Anne Hegnauer

A Short History of Newton Hall, Chester, by Chris Fozzard

Serial Love: When Happily Ever After... Isn't, by Kathy Kay

Sit-Ins, Drive-Ins and Uncle Sam, by Bill Slawter

Black Water and Tulips, by Sara Mansfield Taber

Ghosted: Dating & Other Paramoural Experiences, by Jana Eisenstein

Walking with Fay: My Mother's Uncharted Path into Dementia, by Carolyn Testa

FLAWED HOUSES of FOUR SEASONS, by James Morris

Word for New Weddings, by David Glusker and Thom Blackstone

It's Really All about Collaboration and Creativity! A Textbook and Self-Study Guide for the Instrumental Music Ensemble Conductor, by John F. Colson

ABOUT THE AUTHOR

Alison was Educated in Paris, earned a BA at George Washington University in Radio/TV Broadcasting. President of Salty Water Properties, Inc. she brings a breath of fresh air to the Southern Californian Real Estate market. Alison began writing at an early age and her articles have been published in Moon Tide Media's South Bay Magazine, chronicling the adventurous journeys with her husband Ken until the ultimate journey took his life.

Raised in California, Alison has lived around the world from Canada, Scandinavia, Europe, the French West Indies and the middle East.

Alison calls South Redondo Beach her home. Her daughter Baxter, son-in-law Jack and grandson Angus live in Sonoma.